EXIT ISLAND

Also by Terri Witek

Poetry

Fools and Crows (an Orchises book)

Carnal World

The Shipwreck Dress (an Orchises book)

Criticism

Revising the Self: Robert Lowell and Life Studies

EXIT ISLAND

•

Terri Witek

Orchises

Washington

2012

Library of Congress Cataloging Publication Data

Witek, Terri, 1952-
Exit island / Terri Witek.
p. cm.
ISBN 978-1-932535-25-9 (alk. paper)
I. Title.
PS3623.I86E95 2012
811'.6--dc22

2011011837

Thanks to editors of the following journals who published versions of these poems:

A Bad Penny Review: "At World's End // Double Album," "Faz a Curva Where the Wind Turns Round," "How to Make a Homemade Phonograph," "Night Sky Plus Heteronyms: Teenage Temptation No. 4," "Night Sky Plus Heteronyms: Thrilling Comics No. 5," "Night Sky Plus Heteronyms: Jungle Comics No. 158"
Alhambra Poetry Calendar 2011: "The Day You Left // Swimming Pool"
Blackbird: "How to Apparel Yourself for the Hunt," "Walking Angry"
The Cincinnati Review: "Getting to the Bottom of It"
Connotation Press: An Online Artifact: "How to Mutiny by Hoisting a Sail," "How to Mutiny from the Crow's Nest," "How to Mutiny Via Peg Leg"
The Hudson Review: "After a Calm Day"
Improbable Object: "Um Passeio With Pop Quiz," "& Some Technical Difficulties," "Catullus Quilt," "Cheetah Zone," "Cheetah Zone Night Sky Hurry Up," "Walking Together Their Tails Beside Them"
Journal of the Motherhood Initiative: "Gravel Alley Bottle," "How to Affect an Ice Rescue," "Wet Specimens," "Wood Bottle"
Mezzo Cammin: "The Distance Between Us Tmesis"
new south: "How to Answer as a Homemade Telephone"
New Ohio Review: "I'll Meet You in the Isenheim Altarpiece," "The Exegete"
Saw Palm: "Bottle Blonde," "Hurricane Shade," "20-25 Miles an Hour,""Wave Palinode"
Slate: "The Day You Left // Mammogram"
32 Poems: "What a Day"

My gratitude to Stetson University for sabbatical leave, to Art Sullivan and to Melissa Sullivan for support via the Sullivan Chair in Creative Writing, and to The MacDowell Colony, Hawthornden International Retreat for Writers, Convento São Francisco de Mértola, and the Atlantic Center for the Arts. Thanks especially to Ralph Savarese of Writers@Grinnell and Lesley Wright of the Faulconer Gallery, who commissioned the original collaboration with Cyriaco Lopes, and to Eric DeLuca for his (altered) directions on how to make a homemade phonograph, to Leonidas Dezes for technical help, and to Rusty Witek for the comics.

ORCHISES PRESS
P. O. BOX 320533
ALEXANDRIA, VA 22320-4533

G6E4C2A

for Cyriaco

who visited Ariadne's house and left me a book

CONTENTS

A suite of photographs by Cyriaco Lopes follows.

The above rules depend, of course, upon having sea room. In case land interferes, a vessel should heave to, as recommended for the semi-circle in which she finds herself.

American Merchant Seaman's Manual

I. Premise

I wake on an island. The ship has dropped me here—I can still feel it tugging at the edges of sleep, gray and grainy with rain.

Here is what I was told on the ship:

1. Do your arguing on deck.
2. Thefts are rare.
3. Find out how a windlass works: some day you'll have to get that anchor up or down.

But now I am disembarked. The word shudders over the one who has lost her ship with its strange wooden skin. Or the word could be "desemboca," Portuguese ordering river down into the sea. But I am sleeping, not a native speaker, and things are changed by island ears. I hear "disse sem boca"—speak without a mouth, or maybe "além da boca": beyond the mouth. The book on my chest, turned down on my chest, still rises and falls. "Basta-me que me basta"— enough is enough.

in a sea without sound

each wave's a shadow
gill-breathing continues
run amok, moonbeam
no rest, no rest

in a sea without sound

wingless wave egrets
this echo's an accident
also no sandbar
who dives for the moon?

in a sea without sound

immigration by touch
another deaf island
compulsory drowning
fish fish fish fish

in a sea without sound

end gravity too
storms fade like migraines
no pleasure in weeping
grog all around

in a sea without sound

how will I find you?
fasten one eyelid
how will I find you?
go to pieces, green wave

Ariadne had two husbands, Theseus and Dionysus. The first abandoned her on the island of Naxos, where Dionysus later appears and marries her. There are many renderings of the interval: in them, Ariadne often sleeps. But before she became this sleeper, indeed, before she was married, Ariadne was already half-sister to the Minotaur, himself a banished creature of parts.

What language does Ariadne speak? Under the xenophobic principle "it's all Greek to me" Theseus speaks teutonic English quite powerfully but has trouble deploying prepositions: "with" is one he tends to misuse. His book is a 1938 American Merchant Seaman's Manual, and he is given to instant tutorials and quizzes. His ship, shaped for exploration, curves wood from Brazil: in English the ship's a "man-of-war," in Portuguese a "caravela."

Dionysus speaks only by touch, and prefers toys   piggy bank

magic lantern

toy phone

and musical instruments   saxophone

paper

bronze bowl

to books. Ariadne is not aware of him yet as she stirs on Naxos. She still (ainda) dreams—partly in the language of Theseus (sea-warped thesis or thesaurus), partly in the language of the wood of the ship. And she has washed up on Naxos with the poetry of Fernando Pessoa (person, persona), who speaks as a different man in each book. More and more awake, she reads Pessoa slowly and doesn't look anything up (rather, when she looks up she's observing the island). Because she knows his language so imperfectly, it remixes the junctions of her childhood's green labyrinth. To speak it is to bastardize but not possess (kill) it. To speak it is to make, as her mother once made, the Minotaur.

THE DAY YOU LEFT // SWIMMING POOL

We plunge into the huge, cool fakery
and try to spread it hand by hand:

we nearly touch a sun-stunned moth
and a fringy tree drooped further

into uncertainty by last year's storms.
Does any light lead deeper?

Wild plumbago's trading blue for blue.
And what to make of one small coracle

shellacked with golds and greens,
three thready legs still rowing sky?

Cupped palms, one heave.
Wings try creaking in the weeds.

To the edge we pull away from then,
"I'll be gone the world's blue length," you said.

ALÉM

q. Where am I?

a. Além (Beyond)

q. What am I tripping over when I try to wake up?

a. Rock underwater

a. Rock awash at any stage of the tide

Given that one eye, the forgetting one, plays it close to the vest, stays small. Given that from here no mar with its fault line horizon, no broken tide of the mouth.

No greeting but green. Fanned (given) but no veil, no dingy velvet curtain yanked to burlesque in a banana hat, *Tem Banana na Banda*. The ship depends on frapping line, flares, buoys, subjected people. Today's left eye, opening first, depends on palmetto, the understory, what can be eaten without collapsing into some telenovela loop of how the bus left Arlington without her. How the man said *my puppy's in the car.* A palmetto, one or more handed, fibers by the brown millions curled at the base. Green motionless wavings. The lid palpitating a little—not in memory's exhaustive enumerations (palmetto), not in surprised-in-sand lanterns (palmetto), but in green (verde, verdade) the truth.

fog

horn

bell

fog

trumpet

bird

minute   whistle

Police could pat me down to palmetto

palmetto

palmetto

palmetto

palmetto

palmetto

palmetto

no green card

........stamp what lies prone in each direction HOMELESS

&   I'm sem (w/o)   a coverlet curled   under since girlhood

purple silks   x   with a sleeping girl

figuring   many threads now missing........

CATULLUS QUILT (THE OLD STORY)

when you cover / · girl in love w/ story

50 *uariata figures* 50

91 .... *ex illo* *flagrantia* 91

of girl in love & Greek ~~~ into Latin

92 ....*corpore flammam* 92

plus ~~~~~~~ (not one) Pessoa we are contos

93 *imis .... exarsit* 93

cont - ando ~ contos ~ tales

94 .... *corde furores* 94

telling ~ tales some hotter

51 *xx* *arte ....* 51

In pictures, each floats the sky alone,

its surface marked by steri-strips:

a mole becomes a knob-headed pin,

the scars where miners have gone in, blurred Xs.

By now the vast canals, some silted shut,

seem stonily immune to probes

pinging home faint discomforts.

So we're relieved both worlds include

only the grayish skies they drift through

and just one cupola or darkened hut.

These last, by signaling each other,

can gather, as the great head of Buddha

does from his amazing topknot,

all tender, contradictory feelings.

The drowsy interval between husbands has nearly been denied in Titian's *Bacchus and Ariadne*. There the mortal, arms still swept seaward, half-turns toward a caravan of nymphs and satyrs disporting up a wooded Naxos path. Although her body's torqued for motion (ondas not quite andando) the outcome's in place: an 8-starred constellation, what she'll become through Dionysus, already floats the daytime

sky.

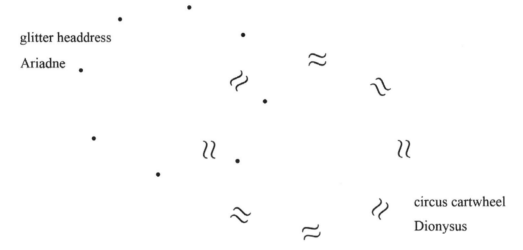

glitter headdress

Ariadne

circus cartwheel

Dionysus

The most inexplicable objects in the charged zone between Ariadne and the leaping Dionysus? Two cheetahs. Captured, perhaps, on a junket to India, they bunch under belled collars, drawing the circus cart through groundswell. Neither pards (leo) nor dandle-heads, they are par: a paired set. A threat? A small dog (drug sniffing from the police station? he doesn't look like a stray) ignores them. They are, after all, impossible. The fastest animals on earth are here the stillest things on the scene. And no one paints cheetahs in 1523. Turned slightly toward each other, they purr both in and out: ronronnar, ronronnar.

q. What is the signal meaning "this is the best place to land"?

a. By day, someone beckoning on the beach.

a. By night, two torches burning together.

So I open my eyes to a trail marker

                palmetto

with these directions:

                eat the heart (feral pigs)

                eat the heart (boars)

                disperse the seeds (all mammals)

and I'm hungry now, not sleepy, not so bound to the waves (ondas) but out walking (andando).
So I follow the trail. And Fernando Pessoa is with me too and in my ear
he breathes very calmly:

      Só quis ver como se não tivesse alma

      Só quis ver como se fosse apenas olhos

                  and I too would like to see
(v [iv] er) as if I didn't have a soul for a minute, I too would like to live as if only
with my eyes. The old unspeakable ties snipped like ceremonial ribbons, yanked
from the bolt. Another trail marker:

                yellow jessamine (poor man's rope)

                good for eye ailments

                toxic to deer

                to honeybees

                native

Then this one, not far from the last (I'm in the thick of it now), a census of the inhabitants:

creatures who will eat anything but can't chew it

creatures fatal only if they keep hanging on

the unseen, biting at dusk and at dawn

I feel cheerful now—more awake. I'm learning island. Yellow jezebel jessamine loops the trail, entrancing. The air's heavy, as if with rain. So what if hunger hoped for something as simple as bread. Like any lost tourist I'll eat palmetto seeds and later disperse them:

        Seed 1: post office

        Seed 2: drugstore

        Seed 3: shop of artisanal wallets and purses

        Seed 4: police station

        Seed 5: burlesque show

The unseen marker for this, visible only at dawn and at dusk:

the new Naxos   nexus   no access

And, to sweeten the path from what's been to what's here

        (só quis ver)

a poor woman's rope

to the future

--------what's next to us.

1 inch Keep Off!
2 inches one may,
3 inches small groups,
4 inches "O. K."!
  Girl Scout Handbook, 1947

Nothing reaches where I've gone under
so no talk, no plank, no red plastic bucket

skidding sideways toward winter's volunteer well.
And don't trust your feet

(the left still taps directions).
Forget the sky's blue distraction.

As bystanders tie themselves
sleeve by wool sleeve together,

count expertly to nine
then redistribute your weight.

Via arms, breasts, genitals and knees,
slide across the opaque skin of the lake,

which may, under this heat,
give way just a little.

Water birds plummet past, laughing.
A doctor's been sent for.

Back on shore?
Blankets. Hot chocolate. Fire in a barrel.

But don't take your eyes from the spot,
now glazing over, once gladly burned through.

HOW TO READ THE PAST IN ONE EYE

Floaters: ...shadows projected onto the retina by
tiny structures of protein or other cell debris
discarded over the years.

In another life, my friend chased paper

into a thousand filigreed drawings.

Fernando P, he calls the person he was then,

and his ouevre just yesterday arrived

in my right eye as knot-riddled twigs,

black sand, and delicate swinging threads

unmoored (they all are) like ink leaving a pen.

Verdict? A "honking big floater."

Or so a head-lamped authority suggests

I'm flood pillowing the drowned again

or the blank behind some long-running movie

whose non-actors heave with such sincerity

they can't be trusted to feign surprise:

Fernando, they're not on the screen, they're in it!

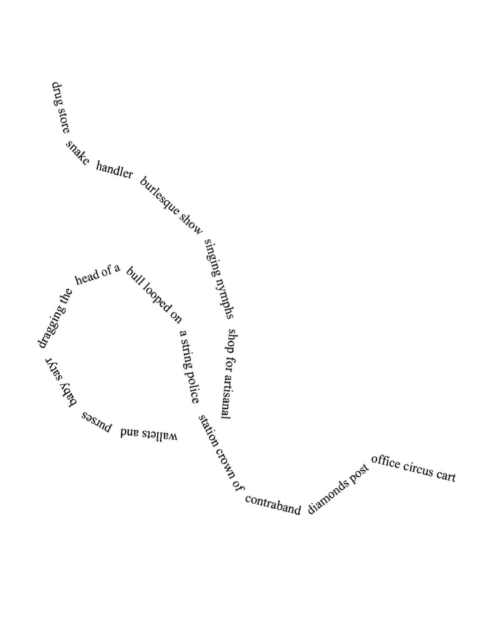

drug store snake handler burlesque show singing nymphs shop for artisanal dragging the head of a bull looped on a string police station crown of contraband diamonds post office circus cart baby satyr wallets and purses

ANCHOR SEA SHANTY

(to the tune of "Drunken Sailor")

What do we swing from sky to island?

What do we swing from sky to island?

…………………………………?

Nada, nada, nada.

Shimmy more chain along the gypsy

……………………………………

Play it out to the bitter end now

Devil's clamp and dear heart.

One wrong swing will cross the cables

Two wrong…… will bend an elbow

Three ………….. will turn her, turn her

Leave her, leave her, leave her.

Pass the dip rope down the hawse pipe

Drop me in the brig with Neptune's daughters

Pass the …..………………

Devil's clamp and dear heart.

What do we sing to a man who's drowning?

How do we hail a ghost ship passing?

…….did we promise Neptune's daughters?

Nada, nada, nada.

BUT I'M NO LONGER SHIP-SHAPE (CONFORME):

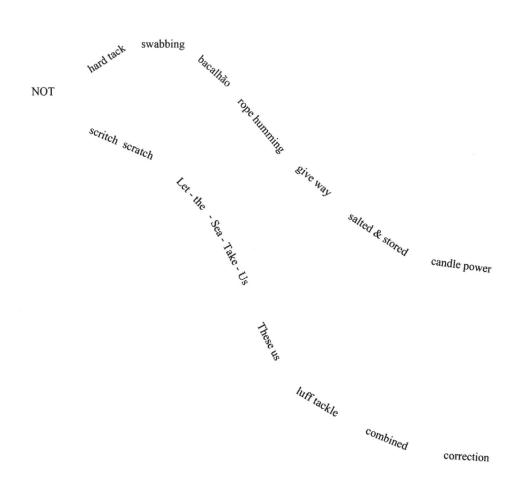

NOT

hard tack   swabbing
bacalhão
rope humming
give way
salted & stored
candle power
scritch scratch
Let - the - Sea - Take - Us
These us
luff tackle
combined
correction

blue

blue

maps

blue

needle

blue

bolt hole

needle

occulting

bale sling

compass

fully insured

onda-lay

onda-lay

lifeboats

and now that I've coughed up the bilge

(+ island satyrs will sate her)   this old saw…..

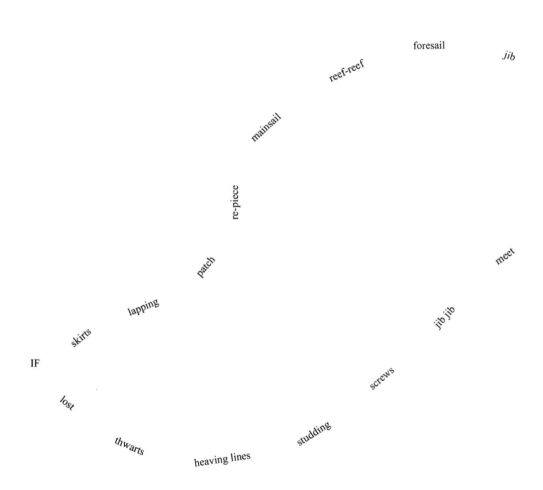

(corollary)

still &

sheet is it   patch

tack

tack   the same   ship

else   where

is

ship 2

Blue Plato

Special   meu

2   capitão

who now

&

commands

both?

q. How am I dressed on Naxos?

a. Neither naked nor nu

q. Vestidada assim?

a. No--em serial greens

q. Does the city offer non-saia options?

a.

drugstore:	strait (white) jacket
sfaw&p:	hoodie
burlesque show:	C note-ruffled G string
police station:	bracelets
post office:	navy blue knee socks

q. What stayed with the ship?

a. White skirt with yellowy sexual stains

a. Menstrual red sunset skirt

a. Plastic grass tutu

a. Blue skirt pulled at the hem

                    (restlessly swabbing)

q. What's gone (saindo) ?

a. Twirling warm spindle self

a. Breeze-whipped flags of backward looking

                    (a little sick-making)

a. Windlass, windlass, windlass, windlass

II. Reverso

I stood on the wharf -- my eyes straining toward the horizon of the sea waiting for Bart's fishing boat to appear when I spotted the dark handsome stranger from the yacht...

HERE -- THAT OUGHT TO BE ENOUGH TO TAKE CARE OF THE BAIT AND SUPPLIES. SEE THAT EVERY-THING IS IN SHIPSHAPE CONDITION FOR TOMORROW.

YES, SIR.

HOW COCKY AND SURE HE IS. SO DIFFERENT FROM ANY OF US HERE IN THE VILLAGE.

Yes -- I envied his confident air -- the manner in which he was used to having people cater to him. And suddenly he was at my elbow...

THEY TELL ME YOU KNOW THE WATERS AROUND HERE LIKE A NATIVE FISH. I WONDER IF YOU'D CONSIDER ACTING AS GUIDE FOR ME AND MY PARTY AROUND THE ISLANDS SOME DAY.

MAYBE!

But my sleep was troubled that night, and early next morning found me pacing on the dock deep in thought when...

MORNING -- I WAS HOPING I'D RUN INTO YOU.

OHHH -- ITS YOU!

(what, in her cups, she thinks really happened)

"Don't break it," he says, and this is a rule like "Retain the handle of the oar in your hand." After the hasty egress, the bird-streaked freshets of wind, we're becalmed. The sea stays gray, sedative silk.

At first, when each unhinged sunset seemed a warning, he staged drills. Two foghorn blasts and we'd rush deckward, grumpy rats in disreputable sleep pants, and lower the boats. Lately he's holed himself up and the crew has splintered predictably into side-betters, novena makers, and those who'll fuck anything. The stowaway finally appears on deck, pressing into his little windowed phone a last declaration or, possibly, our coordinates and SOS. Or just "Oh shit, oh shit, oh shit," what he's saying.

Was the captain (hard to think of him now as the hero) on deck for a sky check when the first bottle bumped astern? Quick, quick. I dipped my hat, scooped. Flicked my catch dry, a flat, clear flask. I've kept it, neck tucked under my sleeve cuff, a twin glass hand. Tonight when I bring him an apple wheeled on a plate and one fish with a shell in its mouth---food arranged for cheer---his voice is an anxious scratch. He suspects where this was going. He knows I'm no drinker.

How to Answer as a Homemade Telephone

Hello, hello.
I'm with some books
on an island.
No—between long wars
and in the aftermath
of revolution.
No, I can't hear you.
I'm only brass,
thin aluminum, and string.
For guts a little wood
and scrumbled pigment.
What? Impossible.
There's no connection.
Though if you could see
my popeyed bells
and bright
unlisted O
of tinfoil fright,
there might be.

GETTING TO THE BOTTOM OF IT

A push-up, shore-up, kick-up dollop—
the bottle's own Davy Jones' locker

keeps it sitting straight at table
but cheats the drinker (what, done so soon?).

Where the blowpipe touched, it's prone
to hold heat, to sag, to play Spin the Bottle.

To make the bottle's Kraken. Its note to itself:
"Remember the time we…" or "Then you said…"

the rest a word balloon or moon that's fallen.
We slink home. Drink too much.

Night blurs through every uncorked bore.
While empties grace the bins with eerie ovals,

handies and slender handies, bevelled ideals,
an orphan Klein bottle touches itself,

stretching mouth so far from body
it loops back through to shape the base.

Dr. Bottle's neither in nor out today.
Hence balance. Hence strength.

Hence a twisting fourth dimension's take
on talking through your ass.

THE DISTANCE BETWEEN US TMESIS

Child (nesting) ren
Book (sticky) plate
Dog (two yards) gone
Third (mortgage) rate

Fact (don't bear) checking
Fore (but won't) play
Foot (no less) binding
Nor (find your) way

To (kiss kiss) morrow
Night (broody) mare
Eye (drawn to) shadow
No (goodbye) where

in which you hoped to

but didn't do much,

dreams can be terrible.

Someone under a streetlight

demands sex,

nakedly raging.

 A woman no one's introduced

coerces you into a walk—

she's amiable,

but the way soon steepens

so you can't really hear her.

You unlatch a gate

(thank goodness, a garden)

but she hangs herself.

Of course the people in dreams

are always you

wanting to be put out of your misery.

But the dream world's huge.

You're the snoring,

dreamless neighbors too

and the phone not dialing 911.

You're the way, the rage,

the rope, the garden.

HURRICANE SHADE

Nothing holds in this wind
(says an hour to its lightest thought).

If the bottom drops out
(says the bottle) I'll house your candle.

Why Put to Sea (The Bottle Factory)

In offshore winds a bottle toots
like a tugboat, hauls us closer in.

We're seven again,
roaming catless Lions Park

where there's no beach either,
just glass so dull we hike it barefoot.

Or is this neolithic sand?
Once (remember, whatever's hot anneals)

factory boys reeled here under trays of bottles,
breaking some into a bay

whose wavering transcriptions
collect this fringe of green stones.

When the new bottling plant opens,
we'll amortize our profit,

oohing syrup rushed down
see-through necks then capped,

reduced to six apiece and gifted
at the exit: Coca Cola.

BOTTLE BLONDE (PROTOTYPE)

Mrs. Smith—the young one, at the other end
of an alley opening like a telescope
down the length of our block—would "rinse"
(another word to like) her entire hair
then lay out on a chaise lounge in shorts
and polka-dotted halter. She stayed landlocked
until late afternoon, when roofers' trucks
grumbled home to their dim garages
and the neighborhood shook as if seen through water.
They carried in what they had carried out:
the Riedy brothers, tar paper rolls, shingles
in gritty oblongs brushed with glitter.
Almost enough to cover Mrs. Smith,
who overhead wanted only summer.

GRAVEL ALLEY BOTTLE

Like low-rent majorettes,
we shared sparklers while the Weikel brothers,

Theodore and Robert, spiked the alley
with roman candles.

Someone's eye fell out.
The clubhouse vanished into embers.

Frowns embossed themselves on brows.
We couldn't say how H2O

in bottle rockets scrubs their flight—
we weren't Newtonians,

(though Chucky Partain,
pitching rocks at a garage-door's

row of dirty diamonds, was.)
Spit! Fetch holy water!

Mrs. Weikel, nurse to a perpetual plummy funk,
broke down and called the fire truck.

The Season For It

Because it was the season for it,
as the sun arrived we touched it.

All day, then, our fingers wore
a little smudge which could be used

(we tried this) like another key.
We didn't once feel hungry,

though as hours gathered
we sometimes brought a hand to mouth

and swallowed embers.
And these lay lightly in us

when we next touched
among the ravished covers.

The investigation links sweat on a boot tongue
to me, a label's lick to you.

Offshore, creatures solder themselves together,
build long, evidentiary reefs

that swiftly confiscate beach.
So though each vintage has its legs, bottle,

we can't run—which in our common delirium
suggests treading water.

Recall that the Civil War amputations
by Dr. Bliss were perfect save for the sepsis.

Another recommendation to stay bottled up:
"All the time he was out of his head

not one bad word or idea escaped him"–
thus Walt Whitman wrote Corporal Irwin's mother

after the boy, wounded near Fort Fisher, succumbed.
Thirty years later a Pennsylvania man

donates a limb which has outgrown him;
it's still a nightmare swagger jamming glass.

After we've been rescued, bottle,
we'll visit it at the National Medical Museum

along with the dry thigh bone of Private Oscar Wilbur,
wounded at Chancellorville, who, as he malingered,

asked Whitman if he "enjoy'd religion"
and was told, at least in the water-rippled

account of this I stole from a library,
"Perhaps not, my dear, in the way you mean."

Trade out one taffeta petticoat the size of a bos'un's headache. Cook will pooh-pooh this "dirty rag"; your shipmates ignore another wind-inked cloud. Eyeing from afar what's aimed at their jetty, shore dwellers will assume black sails mean the end of you and act accordingly.

The lover each of us claims not to keep
combines in this gift of weather,

another fresh-faced recruit
who believes the lie outside our mouths

(cloudless misdirection).
And what ricochets from today's blue dents?

Hope, hope. Our guest,
unwilling to get nice clothes dirty.

Who suspects old habits
ride strapped in the back seat,

sticky and fractious.
Don't look in the rearview mirror, they say.

Stay that long cool drink
you promised yourself after the field trip.

THE EXEGETE

Francesca da Rimini *by William Dyce*

Scottish National Gallery

To say Francesca is untrue to her husband
with Paolo is the first misreading.
The book is her lover.

Because Paolo doesn't know what to do
he kisses her cheek, poor fellow—
it's like touching a child's head.

Her hand kisses the book.
The wall they are sitting on
kisses her through her green skirt.

The museum guard is kissed by a tourist's request
for the exit to Princes Street.
Francesca's husband grasps the wall

from behind--he's climbed up to it,
tracing a page's scent back to his wife,
now leaning gracefully away from this boy

so ardent he yearns toward her
as if into an oblong of light.
The husband will murder them both

for arriving here first and in paint.
Or would (feckless materials!)
except the canvas has been kissed

by a knife so he's only a hand
scrabbling along mossy gray stone
like a disconsolate spider.

Lay an egg. Holding yourself upright, angle the egg overhead like a third, lidless eye. The crew's gaze blunders upward. Bastards, bastards. You are the lighthouse keeper now and this is your warning.

I'LL MEET YOU IN THE ISENHEIM ALTARPIECE

I was looking at Death,

whose T-shaped incision groaned

"Come in. You'll find what you want."

So I unfolded his body

and arrived at a party:

a baby, bright white and gold tassel,

was being hoisted around.

"Didn't you know," Death said,

"if you go in, you'll go up?"

And more things did seem to be

floating now—light cycled through

vaguely nuclear haloes as a band

wove skin after skin of gold sound.

"This isn't how I pictured it,"

I said, and this too was pieced

into the chorus, something about

(was this another language?)

a resurrected heart. I'd gone

a little gaga with light by then,

a twitch tapped behind my left eye.

"Am I dead?" I asked.

"Who questions Death?"

This time the voices rose stiff

and dreadful. I closed my eyes

and saw wheat fields

as if from a car window.

I saw my mother's brown cotton dress

folded into tissue then into a box.

"Please," I said, "let me out."

"You're out of it now," hummed the chorus,

"Look at the baby."

I opened my eyes.

Fields rippled everywhere,

trembling skin of the world,

and light was another skin and birds

were skins over the poisonous grain

they'd already swallowed.

Nearby, the great combines

began gathering hungers.

"Lift me up," I cried then,

and touched, as I passed it,

the look on Death's face, blank and astonished,

and with a great rustling of hinges

a new dark fastened down.

Oh wait, I wasn't pregnant.

Oh wait, you might have wanted children.

1. Fold one of your real legs up like a shorebird does.

2. Whittle a bottle from driftwood; upend and attach.

3. When the watch changes, remove this appendage.

4. Empty into it what you've stolen

5.
                                   scent of damp hammock

                                   doubloon noon

                                   slop-bucket creak

                                   dolphin snout

6. Drop your real leg back down and bind this to its twin.

7. Hoist the peg leg.

8. Leap overboard, mermaid, your new ship in your arms.

THE DAY I LEFT // ETIQUETTE

Unclear if I can come back.
Unclear who would explain: "a mercy"

or "just yesterday she referred to her leg as a tree."
A friend splays fine, pulpy hands as he guesses,

distracted by years of being dead himself.
But now's sun bear still roots blindly through trash.

A bill's little ski chalet opens for guests---
in its lone picture window, fog and no view.

So how (this day must be gotten through)
will I address you

when, with utmost respect, sir,
we each beg to remain, sir,

right honorable atoms,
plenipotentiary ash?

Blind Catch-stitch (breath)

sleep

land

Palmetto Stitch (mente / tiara)

indicates lying (making mentiras)

or just getting in over one's head

Rowing Stitch

also to look downward

FEATHER STITCH (HOW THE GODS MAY STILL BE INFERRED)

biopsy scar + chest hair

wind-filled sails

birds

WOOD BOTTLE (CAPTAIN)

Chasing the ghost of an idea,

I found a solid bottle that displayed,

if I considered too its slanted mouth,

more than one way to be illogical.

But when I claimed a splinter

then tossed the whole contraption shoreward,

I revived a thirst so strange

no tide would suit me.

So I'm glad it's gone beyond me.

Sly undrinkable,

through which the secret grains travel

as if to serve some larger table,

consider me for once less scoffer than I was.

And to all who dislike a crooked span?

Go easy on the bottle, friends.

III. Cheetah Zone

HOW TO APPAREL YOURSELF FOR THE HUNT

Outside, carolling dogs.
In your chest, a slight hissing predicts this year

will not support the great hunts of before,
and it's true your six-toed bitch is gone,

and the half blue-eyed puppies you secretly fed.
A new mount shivers and stamps.

You're thirsty for poison.
But when the fox kindles dry fields,

dreams lie down like neighboring kingdoms.
Your heart with its little hole rejoices.

WALKING ANGRY IN THAT CITY

I swing along like a snake's last rattle,
glad to see windows buckling their bodices

and how, graffittied across piazzas,
each martyr's name spells further torture.

If the shops all seem cacaphonous and crass,
the churches are overly cool and swoony.

Oh, I'm in a right old lather, so high on it
I flail even against a low-slung moon

until, not yet apologetic but sailing into aftermath,
I pass a cat filleting something vague and gray

on the pavement and then (at last)
it is only hunger I too feel.

Belled   only~other   (trespass)   ripple/

ripple   loudspeakers: fog   (pop)   *"Por onde for,*

quero ser seu par"   ////   ser/   not sonho

onda~~sonora   (sum)   quero   cheetah   xx

pulling~   the~cart+   bell   (transfer)   =   guarda

"Por onde for"   *par/ate*   dark-   (IF   EQUAL

UNTIL)   eyeye   (reverse)   plush~touch   3/ 3

(no no)   stroke: dash: transfer   ~ ~ ~ ~   limite

(pass)   (pass)   what's + (hiss)   what's - (hiss)

*Tête Bêche: 1. In bookbinding, two volumes bound together so they have two front
covers and no back cover. 2. In philately, a joined pair of stamps in which one is
upside down in relation to the other.*

In some languages, what will happen
with certainty must be said in the past.
So while we're deciding where to meet up next,
a weary barmaid has already corked up
the bottles and bolted the doors.
And even God's kissed us off,
the way our fathers once smacked us
simply by raising an eyebrow.
No wonder we barely stay home, Fernando:
wherever we go we're already ghosts.

But what of the fabled towns of the past,
terminally estranged from those exburbs
expanding whenever we open our mouths?
At least there's ocean nearby, and a buried reef.
Does the ocean hope to discover the town,
bragging, "Remember the old days? I was your spine!"?
So a girl once saved enough to buy stamps,
so a boy riding a bus shook a book from his satchel
(this happened—you've shown me the book).
But (confesso) I'm still shaken to the root,
Fernando, not to say a little creeped out,
that the girl brushing glue onto blue and green stamps
still puts her money down on the counter
because a woman forty years later unhinges her mailbox!

Maybe speaking by way of the future changes the past,

like eating until the body recalls hunger,

or reading because a particular hour

swerves a well-thumbed book into your hand.

And that past and future rush here from nearly

opposite directions does seem, today,

like new information, or at least a technical advance

in the apparatus which will bring us,

on schedule, to the end of the world.

Which means it also exists in the world's oldest languages.

This isn't one, of course,

though depths may be glimpsed in some syllables

and these have a way of accreting.

But one language can't really hold onto it all

any more than we can hold a thought like this one for long—

which is just long enough, maybe,

for rain to gust in and blur some addresses.

The bus stops again—no one exits.

Did you loan me this book?

It opens to an envelope from Brazil.

No letter, and the stamps have been neatly snipped out,

the way half-closing our eyes edits hills from a view.

See you always and never.

Now I've sent them to you.

(photo by Vik Muniz)

After a lapse (what happened?)
some things, though pinned to dark, seem clear—
whatever untranquil ghosts we shared
return to devil us in this trace of….what?
our lost, caressing bodies?
Translucent footprint, stored space,
that you dangle unaccompanied
twists all we forgot to take true measure of
forever to the same pale crux:
did we need each other even once?
Now, now. Best touch only the graceful
face of things (no less timely or real)
and see what hangs on as sheer material,
the last shocked breaths we'd freely trade.

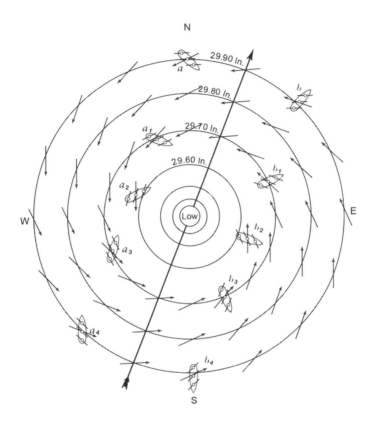

Figure 230. Diagram illustrating rules for maneuvering a sailing ship during a cyclone (Northern Hemisphere).   For Southern Hemisphere, reverse.

1. You are making a funnel but don't go in.
2. Roll so one end's wider.

           Do I tape this thing?

3. Yes. Now pierce the small end

   w/ your needle.

4. Allow half-an-inch

   to stay on the eye side.

5. No, it shouldn't move.

   Tape.

6. Snap a pencil in half.

         In half?

7. That's the tone arm or base

   (let's call it the base).

           Are you in a car?

8. Yes.
9. Duct tape one pencil half

   (eraser end up)

   to the cardboard square.

10. No, so it stays straight up.

        Where are you going?

11. OK, take the speaker and   pick up the thumbtack

                                  jimmy the thumbtack

                                  fix needle and speaker to base

                                  w/ the thumbtack

                                  push thumbtack through one side of cone

                                  to eraser you want the speaker

                                  to teeter-totter on base

12. What? Needle face down and tilting—

it shouldn't touch ground.

13. You holding a record?

14. Classical is shabby.

    Hip hop or pop.

15. Now, pencil 2.

    Insert and shimmy the record up it.

16. Twirl.

17. Clockwise. Guys, keep it down.

17. Clockwise.

18. Well, only if you want to hear

        watch the way Missy like to take it backwards

        a god with hooves, a god with horns

1.

The hemispheres, parting equatorially,
deflate in darkness, cool, then spin.
"Don't follow me,"
a last, pegleg pilgrim mutters,
purrs or hums. What's next?
"Donna Summer" bolds the signage
at one oasis, formerly Antarctica,
no one reaches. "Air raid,"
hisses the space around a central
glinty totem who, classically aloof
from me + you + her + him
but doomed to hear it all again,
turns and turns like any god
faking rescue or couvade.

2.

No strobe from the second lighthouse
which, since waves and world have fused,
ditched its keeper. Are there natives?
What would anybody breathe here,
fossilized, as they seem to be,
 in black macadam (feel it give)?
At least what we loved lies here together.
Unreachable. But something stings
like unredeemed electricity.
So scratch on, constellation's dew claw
or jumpy little pin of wind.
Hum along with waking voices
who don't insist where home may be:
"It's sweet (so sweet) to die in the sea."

WHAT A DAY

Names held firm, of course, and the sea
was still breakingly the sea,
but somehow the slightest word expanded,

turned tea kettle, turned pipe organ.
A few swore themselves to silence.
But soon the ragged cries of love returned

so clear, so gorgeously mended,
we thought birds must be trapped in the houses
though we could still see birds

teetering in the grass, beaks open.
A little wildly, then, we tried to signal
by eyelash, by pockets turned out,

by dancing, but even the gods
wandered back, tricked out in faded
rock star gear and twirling guitars—

the day relaxed,
extending into a huge, migratory party
where no one ate a thing but air

and this might have meant
the last of us, Fernando,
but "the end" is words, so nothing ended.

WAVE PALINODE

They don't love us as we love them.
Yet from beleaguered shorelines
each rolling flank of gold and green
conceives of the world continuing.

How we loved, when young and breeding
within quickening hills of pleasure,
to think the world so needed us
we could outride its will and measure.

Still reading outside at a strange day's end,
I watched words drag their shadows

until one leaf braced a spider opening further
into a maelstrom of tiny, upside-down *L*s.

Which startled a little hunter anole
tricked out in identical brown leaf color.

He belled his throat (having swallowed
what was left of the sun) to show he knew

the possible end of a pas-de-deux.
But at least they were full of each other,

lizard and spider mother.
And when, sleepless and changing

one plot for another,
we were drawn to that night's upward bloom

"Don't pause" was the only cloud-thought crossing
what rounded between the Star Crab's claws.

Nogueira Pessoa	fog bell
Navas	fog gun
Alberto Caeiro	fog horn
Ricardo Reis	fog siren
Inspector Guedes	fog trumpet
A. A. Crosse	fog whistle
Pipa Gomez	bird
Pantaleão	minute

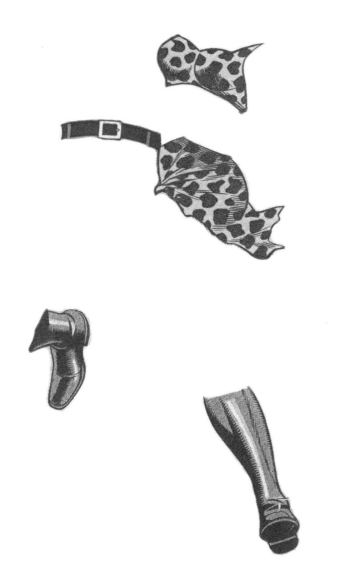

So   boy   beach   draw-the-airplane   I'll   but

U.S.   tinfoil   county road   fast   so   flick

(*Os Paqueros*)   red + white   song   convertible

blonde +   blue   hat   orange hat   banana

hat   bikini   pregnant   (*Todas as*)   photo

(*Mulheres*)   crash   Fernando   finger   screen

air   belly   "met her"   not   not

Ipanema   but   daughter   black socks

sunburn   blue   tuning forks   quivering

Regime change.

The eyes not sufficient now. The mind not.

Nor tiny green voices

                         palmetto seeds

thrumming into my ears—I yank them out

(a series of small objects falling).

Enter a barred owl cruising its 8th note,

                        the victim.

Enter a 13-year trial by cicada

and the last rule of the labyrinth:

                    go forward and down.

Then casually, like moon shifting the sea's buck and hiss,

enter something

                    o que

not the sum of its parts

                    o som

and not death

though death is bent into it

like gull's cries are tucked into weeping women.

Enter

                    for once, traceable

                    for once, w/o the eyes' frantic searchlights

                    an old saw sem sorrow

                    go forward and down

5 seconds whistling

         my lover

3 jingly bracelets

         my lover

1 moon-stricken fruit
sighing 8 purple berries

         ....
         night's perfect pitch.

Nipples at Two Latitudes

Dionysus and Ariadne by Tullio Lombardo

NIGHT SKY　　　　(CHEETAH ZONE // HURRY UP)

.　.　　　.　　.　　　　.　　　.

.　.　　.　　.　　.　　.

American Merchant Seaman's Manual

Ariadne on Naxos (Opera in One Act)

Collins Portuguese-English Dictionary

Nietszche's Dithyrambs of Dionysus,

and all the volumes of Pessoa's poetry close, tangling their limbs across dark reef:

indicator.   //   capsizing. This subject is discussed later.

Will music soothe her pain?   //   ECHO

sonho (soh' nyoo) m.   dream   //   that; tirar 'a_____, to draw lots

Ich bin dein Labyrinth ...   //

FIG. 1   FIG.2   FIG. 3   //   repeated until all are landed

& already the newest curve of moon is rising........is this too my husband?

bearing

round

sounding

known

angle

sextant

three known

objects

Appear.
I say this and a bee,
buzz-headed phoneme, wobbles in,
shakes out the dust from—what? Crowned vetch?
Mint? Purple clover? Memory's
small-scale deliriums.

Appear.
This time an unframed mirror
(did I say, Fernando, the scene
extends to a mirror and some chairs?)
rounds completely into green.
I won't say this again:

Appear.
Or stay as you are,
chafing the sting of what's been,
while another loiterer moves through, move on.
A breath. A breath. A breath.
I'm gone.

WALKING TOGETHER THEIR TAILS BESIDE THEM (LOVE POEM)

TO FERNANDO FROM SILENCE

My window widens to treetops.
Meters down, white feathers

spell last night's tragedy,
but the world's not sad, for once,

nor hungry. I hoped to describe
the dizziness which comes on

when I change books under this canopy
the sky keeps raising,

but you already know and the symphony's
started—rain and me reading you

in ways so sweet and unexpected
they've opened my mouth.

IV. THE VOYAGE OF THE MINOTAUR

CARAVELA WITH TWO LINES BY FERNANDO PESSOA

Cresce a vinda da lua   (but what is gained by the moon's return?)
                    Teu corpo, teu limite.

When will o rio dovetail nas ruas   and which ainda arrives too soon?
                    Cresce a vinda da lua.

While the drunken dogwatch pities   another far-off monsoon,
                    Teu corpo, teu limite.

Something pulls against day's patois.   Something restrings the body's loom.
                    Cresce a vinda da lua.

Who would leave your side for comfort?   Who would row against the moon?
                    Teu corpo, teu limite.

Tudo cresce, tudo pity   tudo rua, tudo moon
            all is body, all is rowing,   all notation is natação.

The suite of seven images on coated stock
was created by Cyriaco Lopes
in response to Terri Witek's *The Shipwreck Dress* and *Exit Island.*

Twenty-six copies of this book,
lettered A through Z and signed by the author and artist,
are available from Orchises Press.

———

Each volume contains one color image from the *Exit Island* suite printed on aluminum.

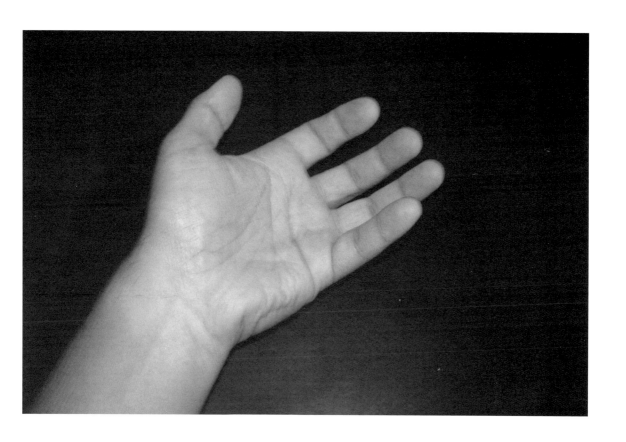

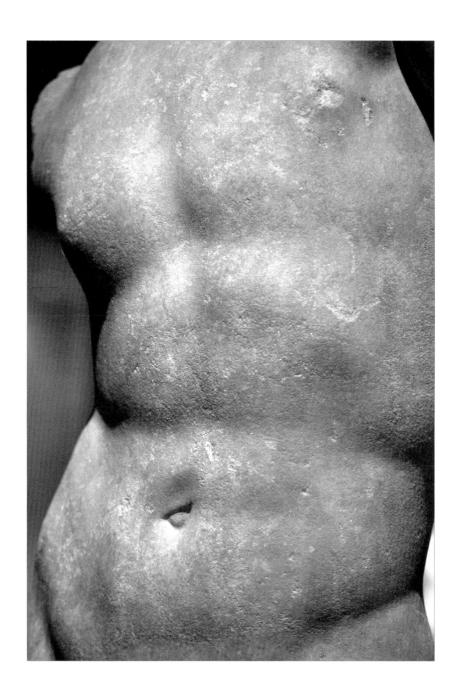